Air Plants

LOUISE HARVEY

CONTENTS

INTRODUCTION TO AIR PLANTS

There are over 550 different varieties of air plants found today. These flowering plants have the scientific name Tillandsia. They are part of the Bromeliad family and are in fact related to Ananas Comosa, or the pineapple to you and me!

The Bromeliad family consists of three specific groups. They are Bromelioidea, Pitcarinioideae and Tillansiodea (from which Tillandsia or air plants originate). Tillansiodea are the only sub-family whose leaves contain a smooth edge.

Tillandsia, or air plants, come in all shapes, sizes, forms and varieties and are unique in the fact that they develop and grow without the need for soil. They can grow on rocks, trees, bushes, shrubs and sometimes cacti using their roots as a form of anchoring system. In the home environment, air plants are often grown in glass containers called terrariums.

Air plants that grow on rocks are called epipetric plants and obtain nutrients from decaying plant matter around them, including their own dead leaves, as well as from rain water. Air plants that grow on other organic matter are called epiphytic and they obtain nutrients from decaying plant and animal matter as well as air, rain and other forms of moisture.

Air plants leaves contain either hairs or scales called trichomes. These actually help to feed the plant by absorbing any water and nutrients the plant encounters. Air plants are not parasitic in anyway and never use nutrients from the plants that they are attached to. They are found mostly in Central and South America, the Caribbean and in some southern areas of the United States.

Air plants generally flower once only. Depending on the type of air plant, flowers may last anything from 2 weeks up to a year. Flowers come in a range of colors including purple, pink, yellow, orange and red. Air plants flower at the end of winter and can carry on deep into summer.

Outside air plants may become pollinated while in bloom. If this happens they will produce seed pods. These pods contain many tiny seeds which are naturally dispersed in the breeze. It is possible to cultivate an air plant from these seeds but it takes 2 to 4 years and is fairly difficult. The plant has another way of reproducing. This is vegetative in origin and starts when the plant produces small baby plants (called pups), around its base. Once matured, which takes a varying amount of time depending on the species, these can be removed and tended to as a new air plant. Alternatively, they can be left attached to the adult forming a bigger plant. In turn the pups will mature into an adults, flower and produce their own pups. Air plants generally live for around 8 years.

When I started out gardening, these were the first plants suggested to me to try and grow. They are incredibly hardy and relatively easy to grow, which is the perfect combination for beginners. You will still need to keep an eye on them however.

In this book you will learn how to create the perfect environment for your air plant to thrive, how to mount and divide them, how to water and feed them, and finally how to deal with pests and diseases.

At the end of the book I've provided some resources that I've found useful to take my knowledge and understanding to a new level.

THE AIR PLANT FAMILY

With over 550 species and counting, deciding on which air plant to grow can be a daunting task. Luckily, air plants are easy to grow, and if you read this book and follow the instructions, you should not have too many problems growing your first air plant, even if it's your first time.

Selecting your first Air Plant

Let's look at a selection of air plants that are most commonly found at nurseries.

- **Aeranthos**

  Originating in South America, specifically in Argentina, Brazil, Paraguay and Uruguay, Aeranthos is an epiphytic air plant that grows mostly on trees. They can grow both as a single plant or groups of between 2 to 12 plants.

  Aeranthos is characterized by lengthy gray leaves which are extremely pointy. They produce a beautiful deep blue three petal flower and can form many pups. This plant tends to thrive in an area with low humidity and can survive in colder temperatures and is one of the easiest air plants to cultivate although it is fairly slow growing.

- **Bergeri**

  Originating in Argentina, Bergeri is an epiphytic air plant that grows on rocks near the ground. Bergeri produces pups throughout the year and is the fastest growing air plant available.

  Bergeri is characterized by gray to mid green scaly leaves. They produce blue and white flowers containing 3 petals. This plant will thrive in areas that are not too cold, contain excellent air circulation and receive proper light.

- **Ionantha**

  A very common species these air plants originate in Nicaragua and some parts of Mexico. This plant produces white bracts with beautiful blue, red, purple, red and white flowers that grow out of them. The leaves of the plant are often a grey/green color but as flowering approaches they turn a shade of red at the centre of the plant.

- **Purpurea**

  An extremely beautiful air plant found in Peru, Purpurea develop long leaves that spiral around the centre of the plant. The leaves are around 6 inches long and triangular in shape. They taper into a point at their ends and are mostly gray in color. The flower spikes produced by the plant grow around 6 inches tall. Purpurea produces fragrant flowers that smell like cinnamon. The flowers are white lined with purple edges.

CREATING THE PERFECT AIR PLANT ENVIRONMENT

Air plants are very similar to most other plants. They will flourish in the correct environment. Luckily, as gardeners, we have the power to control certain variables that will help to create the perfect environment.

The variables that we need to take into consideration are light, air circulation, temperature and humidity.

Light

Air plants are no different to all other plants! They need light, but definitely in the correct amounts. For a general guideline, plants that have thicker, tough, greyish color leaves can be exposed to more light than those that have thinner, greyish/green leaves.

Indoor air plants need to be placed in an area that receives natural, bright, diffused light (if possible). It should be no further than around 3 to 5 foot from this light source. A window, skylight or clear glass door all make excellent choices as a light source providing filtered sunlight. Outdoor air plants should be kept in a shaded area but still near enough to natural light. The air plant should not get too much sun however, as this will damage it in the long term. Some early morning or late afternoon sun can be acceptable coupled with a high humidity.

Air plants can also grow under artificial lights including fluorescent lights or LED's. The air plant should be placed around 10 – 30 inches from the light source. An air plant growing under artificial light should receive around twelve hours of light per day. Never use halogen or incandescent lights as they produce too much heat which will over time end up damaging the plant if it is placed too close to the light source.

Air Circulation

Air plants need to be placed in an area that has adequate air circulation. There are two main reasons for this. Firstly, the plant is able to take nutrients out of the air through its trichomes. Secondly, the moving air plays a critical part in helping to dry the plant after watering. The plant must dry out properly, especially near the bottom of the plant where all the leaves collect. Any water left here will start to rot the plant. Air movement also helps to keep an air plant cooler in times of extreme heat.

Areas that have a lack of air circulations might also encourage pests to attack the air plant.

Air movement can come from a number of sources. In the case of indoor plants, place the air plant in an area where natural air movement occurs in the house. This can come from an open window or even a draught that moves through the house when certain windows or doors are open, creating air circulation.

Obviously, for outdoor air plants, air circulation is provided by a natural source, the wind!

Temperature

Air plants grow in a range of temperatures in the wild and the same is true for your air plants at home. A good idea is to keep them in an area that has a temperature of between 50 to 90 degrees Fahrenheit with no more than a 10 degree drop at night, if possible. Air plants will certainly thrive when kept in this range. They can be kept in higher temperatures but will need to be watered more regularly.

Cold temperatures over an extended period of time are detrimental to the health of an air plant. Air plants can survive exposure to light frost but will suffer damage. If they are exposed for a long period of time however, they will die.

Humidity

Unlike many other plants, humidity does not play a massive factor in the proper growth of an air plant. It cannot, however, be ignored. The air plant uses its trichomes to remove humidity out of the air as a way of feeding itself in the wild. Humidity levels of 40% - 50% should be perfect for most air plants. Plants that are in areas with a lower humidity will need to be watered more often and those that are in high humidity areas, less often.

If you live in a climate that is relatively dry and with fairly low humidity, you could make a tray to help raise the humidity level around the air plant. To make one, simply take an open container, place rocks and small stones into it. Add a little water to the bottom, around 15mm deep. Place it under, or near your air plant, but do not let any part of the air plant touch the water. As the water evaporates, it creates humidity that your air plant will absorb through its trichomes.

WATERING AND FEEDING YOUR AIR PLANT

A friend of mine approached me a few years ago with a problem. She could not understand why her Aeranthos air plant was not growing; in fact it seemed to be dying. I went to have a look and the poor thing was in a terrible condition.

She explained to me exactly how she looked after the plant. At the end of everything I asked her if she had left something out. She was convinced she hadn't. "What about water," I asked her. "Why would they need that? They live on air!" was her reply.

I am always amazed that so many people think this way. **ALL** plants need water and an air plant is certainly no different, although they are extremely hardy and can go without water for a period. This will seriously hamper their development and they will eventually die.

Remember, an air plant also does not receive nutrients from the soil as other plants do and therefore correctly watering your air plant is critical if you want a healthy plant.

Watering your Air Plant

Each species of air plant will generally require different amounts of moisture to ensure optimum growth. There a few general trends to follow that can help to ensure a healthy plant.

- A general rule is to soak the air plant in water at least once a week. Plants with green colored leaves need watering more often than their gray and silver leafed counterparts.
- An air plant in need of water will display leaves that are very light in color, and either wrinkled or rolled up. If the air plants leaves are stiff and plump it is been watered correctly.

- The best method to water the plant is to submerge it in a container of water for between 20 to 30 minutes. If you live in a very dry area, the plant can be submerged for a bit longer. Do not leave it for too long however, unless your air plant will not have access to water for some time, such as when you go away on holiday. If this is the case, soak the air plant for a 12 hour period.
- Young air plants can be hydrated by placing them in the water and taking them out several times.
- Be sure to remove any excess water by shaking the plant.
- Ensure that the plant is dry around 4 hours after watering; especially the centre section near the base. If this is left wet, rot can set in. Sufficient light and air circulation will help the plant to dry properly. It is best to water your plant in the morning as this will also ensure it has more time to dry. Plants should never dry too quickly however as then they are not hydrating properly.
- Air plants can be misted with a sprayer in between regular watering. This is especially true for areas that are hot, dry and less humid. Air plants kept near air conditioners should also be misted frequently.
- Air plants that are flowering should not be submerged in water. They can be rinsed under running water, paying particular attention to not damage the fragile flowers.
- Water quality is extremely important. Never use water containing chemicals such as chlorine, magnesium salts, calcium or chalk as these will block the trichomes on the leaves and stop them from taking up nutrients. If you are unsure, rather water your air plant with rain, bottled or spring water with a pH level of between 4 and 8. Never water your air plant with distilled water as it contains no nutrients at all. The water should also be kept at around room temperature.
- Watering also serves a secondary purpose. Because of their texture, air plants hold a lot of dust. Watering will help to remove this.

Feeding your Air Plant

Although you can feed your air plant fertilizer, they do not need too much. Air plants absorb nutrients during the process of photosynthesis and by drawing in carbon monoxide. Fertilizers will help to encourage a plant to flower while also helping to strengthen it. Apply the following rules when using fertilizers on your air plant.

- Feed your air plant a fertilizer formula around once a month.
- Use a Bromeliad fertilizer with a 17-8-22 ratio but dilute to around ¼ or ½ strength. Alternatively you can use orchid fertilizers but again it should be diluted to around ¼ strength.
- Either spray the plant with the diluted fertilizer or alternatively, the plants can be soaked.
- Fertilizers containing copper, or zinc should not ever be used on air plants.
- As part of your watering routine, soak your air plants in pond water, if available. This is a natural way of fertilizing the plant as it draws in the nitrates present in the pond water.

DIVIDING AIR PLANTS

When your air plant develops pups you have two options. Either let them stay with the original plant or you can remove them and let them grow by themselves.

If you choose to remove them, be sure to follow these few easy steps.

- **Divide at the right time**

  Pups will emerge just after the plant has flowered. Initially they look like small buds but if left alone, will grow into air plants of their own. I like to wait until the plant has produced a few pups before I begin to divide the air plant up. If you decide to remove a pup, make sure that it is at least half as big as its parent plant.

- **Detach the anchor root**

  Use a sharp knife to loosen the roots of the pup from the area where they are attached to the main plant. You should not have to cut them, they should come free easily enough.

- **Detach the pub from the main plant**

  Using a sharp knife, trim the pup as close as you can to the base of the main plant.

- **Select the location for the pup**

  Decide where the pub will grow. Will you mount it? Will you attach it with some string and tie it outside? Whatever you choose, give the pup a chance to establish itself in its new environment.

AIR PLANT GARDENING TOOLS

With air plants been relatively easy to grow, you do not need a large number of tools to cultivate them. I would suggest that you would have most of these already in your garden shed, although if you are very new to gardening, then you might not. The good news is that the tools you need will not cost you too much money. More to spend on air plants then!

These are some of the basic tools you should have to get you started:

- **Small Garden Cutter**

  Although you will not have to cut your air plant often, it is still necessary to have a decent cutting tool for the times that you will. A normal small garden cutter will be perfect. This can be used to trim any dead leaves from the plant, using a diagonal cut. Air plants only use their roots to connect themselves to trees etc. If you prefer that your plants roots are trimmed away, you can do this with a cutting tool as well. Always sterilize the cutting tool after use. This helps to stop any diseases spreading between plants. The easiest way to sterilize the cutting tool is to clean it with cotton balls or paper towel which have been soaked in some rubbing alcohol.

- **Spray Bottle**

  A spray bottle can be used to mist your air plants between watering. This is particularly true in extremely dry climates. Remember to not to use tap water, but bottled, spring or rain water instead.

- **Long handled tweezers**

  These are perfect for gripping small pups and air plants and can be used in a variety of ways. It also helps you to stop handling the plant.

- **Fertilizer**

  As we discussed earlier, air plants do not need fertilizer, but they do encourage flowering as well as strengthening the plant. I've found the best fertilizer to use is one specifically for Bromeliad diluted to ¼ strength.

- **Mounting equipment**

  You may want to secure your air plant to a tree or fence outside. To do this you will need to mount it in some fashion. This can be done in a number of ways, including wire, pins, a waterproof glue (not superglue) or string.

- **Terrarium**

  An alternate way to display your air plant is to place it in a glass bowl or terrarium. These come in all shapes and sizes and are perfect for indoor and outdoor use.

MOUNTING AND DISPLAYING YOUR AIR PLANT

As we have learnt, air plants do not need soil to live. Therefore you **NEVER** put your air plant in soil and in a pot. It will die very quickly.

I must confess, I do sometimes put my air plants in a pot, but they are never buried in any kind of soil and often just sit on top of a base of materials that fill the pot. I normally use a variety of different sized stones and pebbles. The trick in this situation is to find a way to secure the air plant properly.

Mounting your Air Plant

The perfect way to display air plants is to mount them. You can use anything to mount them on, and they will grow on almost anything.

How exactly is the best way to mount your air plant? Well, firstly you will need a few things before you start.

- The air plant you would like to mount.

- Mounting material.

- Glue (a waterproof glue, remember your air plant will be watered often).

- Wire or string.

- A drill.

- A label (to name your air plant).

Now that you know exactly what you will need to mount your air plant, let's look at an easy, step by step mounting method.

- **Decide on the material you will use to mount your air plant to**

  The great thing about air plants is that they can be mounted on anything. It really is up to your personal taste or even your imagination. I like to use pieces of bark, driftwood, rocks and even outside trees. If you are going to use driftwood, remember to soak it thoroughly first. This will help to remove the salt in the wood which can be detrimental to your air plant. Other mounting materials include ceramic tiles, seashells or even a piece of coral. When you have decided the preferred material for mounting make sure you check the size. Remember, your air plant will grow, so take that into consideration.

- **Prepare the air plant for mounting**

  Make sure your air plant looks in the best condition possible when you mount it. This can be done by removing any leaves that are either dead or in the process of dying. Now, not only will your air plant look incredible once mounted, but more importantly, the glue will stick to the plant and the mounting material easier.

- **Positioning the air plant**

  Take your time with this step and work out exactly where to put the air plant on the mounting material. Try different positions and angles and find which you like best. I always try to find the best looking part of my air plant and make sure that is the main part displayed.

- **Drill a hole in the mounting material**

  Why drill a hole? Well, this allows you to hang your air plant should you wish to display it on a wall or something similar. Even if you are not going to display it in this way, rather drill the hole, so you have the option to change at a later date if you desire.

- **Glue the air plant to the mounting material**

  Place some glue on the mountain material and mount the air plant. This is done by pushing the base of the plant onto the glued area until it has set. Ensure that the glue hardens and sets properly. You may need to find a way to prop the plant against something to hold it in place to ensure this.

  Use a glue that is waterproof and free of any toxins that might damage the air plant. Superglue is not suitable.

- **Label and hang**

  Take some wire and thread it through the hole that you drilled. You can now hang your air plant. You may also want to attach a label to remember which air plant it is. If you are anything like me, you will soon have fifty air plants whose names you cannot remember!

Other Display Methods

There are a few other ways that I like to display my air plants both inside and outside.

- **Hanging them with a fishing line**

  This is a perfect way to display your air plants outside. Attach them to a fishing line and hang them from fences, posts, poles, in a greenhouse or wherever you like. Just remember to take the sun into consideration. I have hung a few under some shade netting in the corner of my garden where I have just let them grow, not removing the pups at all. They became extremely big over time and look beautiful.

- **Air plant terrarium**

This is a perfect way to display your air plants both indoors and outdoors. I display a few of my air plants this way, but mostly only indoors.

Remember, no soil! I like to use pebbles, small pieces of wood and even different color beads to decorate my terrarium. I like to use a pair of long handled tweezers when placing my air plants in the terrarium. Always try to put the plant in root first, this ensures the leaves do not get caught on the edge of the terrarium. When taking your plant out to water it, try to position it so that you remove it root first for exactly the same reason.

Plants in a terrarium should be removed to water them. This ensures that no water remains behind in the terrarium which will end up causing rot.

PESTS AND DISEASES

Luckily air plants are not affected by many pests or diseases, but there are a few that you should be on the lookout for.

Pests

There are two major pest concerns for air plants, these are:

- **Mealy Bugs**

   These white bugs are fairly flat, white in color and without wings and look similar to extremely small balls of cotton. They attach themselves to the air plant and drink the sap. They generally congregate in the area where the stem and leaves meet up, sometimes out of sight.

   If you maintain proper watering and the leaves of your plant start to look sickly, turn yellow and sometimes fall off, check thoroughly for a mealy bug infestation. If one of your plants has a mealy bug infestation, immediately place it in quarantine to stop the spread of these pests.

   A natural way to stop mealy bugs is the use of lady bugs, they're a predator in nature. They can also be treated with insecticide. I'm referring to the mealy bugs, not the lady bugs!

- **Scale insects**

   These can often be found all over your air plant, normally underneath leaves. They are similar to mealy bugs in that they attach themselves to the plant and drink the sap from it. They are fairly small and they will look like small light or dark brown bumps on the underside of the leaves. Scale insects cause leaves to turn yellow and fall off. The infected plant should be removed from others and placed in isolation.

Scale insects are more difficult to remove than mealy bugs. If the infestation is light, you can remove them with a tweezer. Alternatively you can dab them with a cotton bud soaked in rubbing alcohol. If the infestation is heavier, consult with a professional at your local nursery for the best insecticide to remove them.

Diseases

There is only one major disease that can affect your air plant.

- **Rot**

  This can appear in two forms.

  Dry rot occurs when your plant is not placed in an area with proper air circulation for an extended period of time, while wet rot is a result of watering your air plant and not let it dry properly. Of these two diseases, wet rot is far more common and by the time you notice it, it may be too late to save your air plant. Check the base near the stem of the plant regularly, make sure it is not becoming soft. This is often an indication that the plant is suffering from rot.

  To prevent rot, always water in the morning and more importantly, make sure your air plant dries properly. To ensure this, shake off any excess water and place it in an area where there is proper air circulation and light. Do not place it in direct sunlight. This ensures that water does not accumulate in the center region of the plant.

  If you keep your plants outside, place them at an angle that encourages the water to flow out of the middle of the plant when it rains.

COMMON AIR PLANT MISTAKES

Although air plants are very forgiving, as a beginner you will still make blunders while caring for them. In this chapter, we will look at a few common mistakes.

Location

The location of your air plant can have a bearing on its health. As discussed in early chapters, your air plant needs sufficient light as well as proper air circulation. Never keep your air plant outside in temperatures below 45 degrees Fahrenheit.

Watering

Watering your air plant properly is of the utmost important. It is imperative that the air plant receives enough water. If the leaves droop and start to fall off, your air plant is probably dehydrated. If this is the case, you need to soak it for a period of around six hours. Continue with a normal watering schedule after this, but monitor the plant to see that the initial soaking was enough.

Of course, not drying your plant properly after watering can lead to rot. Ensure the plant is dried properly after every watering session to prevent this.

Over Fertilizing

Air plants barely need any fertilizer, but as we learnt in an early chapter, fertilizer can help to make an air plant bloom as well as strengthen the plant. However, never over fertilize the plant as this can end up killing it.

A general rule it to fertilize your air plant once a month.

SUMMARY

Growing air plants is a great way to start your gardening career and hopefully will lead you to many successes, firstly with growing these amazing plants and later, plants that are more difficult to grow. Who knows, maybe the gardening bug might bite so deep that you will move onto growing more difficult flowers and plants like orchids or bonsai trees.

Air plants are extremely tough and do not die very easily. With that said, they aren't indestructible and I have lost a few over the years. The secret is never to take it personally, carry on striving to become a better gardener and to continue learning as you go along.

I believe that in this book, I have given you enough information, knowledge and tips to grow your first air plant successfully. Please have fun while doing it, don't get too worried if things are going wrong. If you feel you need advice, don't be afraid to ask at your local nursery.

Remember, first and foremost you should always be having fun! I wish you every success.

RESOURCES

The following websites are ones that I use and recommend. They will help you learn more about air plants.

- Air Plant City

  http://www.airplantcity.com/

- Air Plants

  http://plants.web-indexes.com/airplants/

- Tillandsia International

  http://www.airplant.com/

- Air Plants 4 U

  http://www.airplants4u.com/

- Air Plant Design Studio

  http://www.air-plants.com/

ABOUT THE AUTHOR

Louise Harvey has been gardening for most of her life. She initially spent time in the garden to be close to her mother, but it wasn't long before she had got the bitten by the gardening bug herself.

Her mother gave her a corner of the garden to look after and she used her patch to grow flowers and vegetables. Once she had used up all of the space, she started filling up her bedroom with house plants and taking over the rest of the family home. Louise's mum gradually gave me more space to work with in the garden and eventually shared the entire backyard with her.

She hasn't stopped since. The main difference now is that she has her own home and garden to work on, and her mother has her own one back.

Louise vows to continue learning and experimenting in the garden for as long as possible. She enjoys trying out new methods for optimal growth and isn't afraid to make mistakes along the way. She confesses to making thousands of mistakes in her time in the garden, and she's keen to pass on what she's learned to amateur gardeners alike.

Gardening has changed her life forever. She finds it relaxing, fun, and hugely rewarding. She would like everyone to discover the same benefits.

She's helped numerous friends, family members and colleagues with their home and garden, and she wants to reach out to help more people. Her books are quick reference guides that are simple to understand, fun to read, and provide the amateur gardener with the basic information they need to start gardening.

OTHER BOOKS BY LOUISE HARVEY

Your First Orchid - A Beginners Guide To Understanding Orchids, Growing Orchids And Orchid Care

Your First Cacti - A Beginners Guide To Cacti and Succulents

Your First Bonsai - A Beginners Guide To Bonsai Growing, Bonsai Care, and Understanding The Bonsai

Herb Gardening - A Beginners Guide To Growing Herbs At Home

Composting - The Complete Guide To Composting and Creating Your Own Compost

Self Sufficient Living - A Beginners Guide To Self Sufficient Living and Homesteading

CPSIA information can be obtained at www.ICGtesting.com
Printed in the USA
BVOW06s1041030416

442785BV00029B/453/P